Six Pots

By Debbie Croft

A man has lots of pots at his van.

Tim, this is yam and red fig.

The pots are not big,
so Mum gets six pots
in a box.

Tim and Mum sit
the six pots in the hot sun.

A big can is at the tap.

Tim can wet the six pots.

Mits runs and laps
at the can.

Mits digs in the mud.

Mits hits the pots!

Tim can not fix the pots.

Mits is sad, but Tim
pats him.

9

CHECKING FOR MEANING

1. Where did Mum and Tim buy the six pots? *(Literal)*

2. How did Tim water the pots? *(Literal)*

3. Why do you think Tim patted Mits even though he had broken the pots? *(Inferential)*

EXTENDING VOCABULARY

yam	What sounds are in this word? If you change the *a* to *u*, what new word do you make?
yet	What does *yet* mean? Talk about what Mum means when she says, "*No yams yet!*" Explain that this indicates some yams will grow at a later time.
yip	What does the word *yip* mean in this book? What other words could the author have used that have a similar meaning?

MOVING BEYOND THE TEXT

1. Why did Mum and Tim put the pots in the sun? What do plants need to be able to grow?

2. Why do you think Mits ran to the pots when Tim was watering them?

3. Why do you think Mum bought the pots?

4. What are some plants that you could grow in your garden at home?

SPEED SOUNDS

| Xx | Yy | Zz |

| Kk | Ll | Vv | Qq | Ww |

| Dd | Jj | Oo | Gg | Uu |

| Cc | Bb | Rr | Ee | Ff | Hh | Nn |

| Mm | Ss | Aa | Pp | Ii | Tt |

PRACTICE WORDS

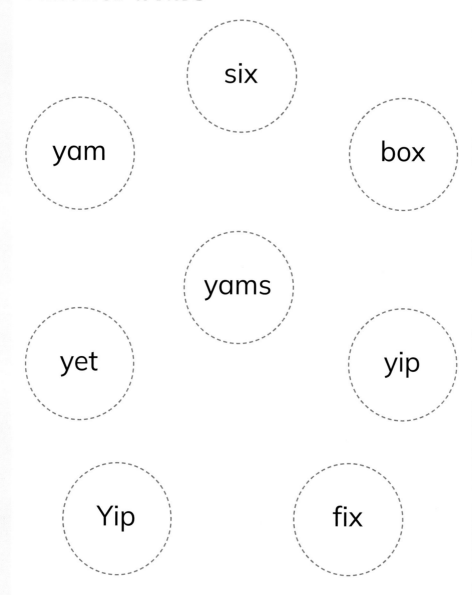

six

yam

box

yams

yet

yip

Yip

fix